ANGELS AND OGRES

BY
JODY MITCHELL

2/9/2014
My darling Christine.
I love you!!
Love
Jody Mitchell

Pending Copyright by Jody Mitchell

No part of this publication may be reproduced, stored in a retrieval system, or transmitted in any form or by any means, electronic, mechanical, photocopying, recording or otherwise, without written permission of the publisher. For information regarding permission, contact Vook.com.

Library of Congress Cataloging-in-Publication Data is pending

ISBN 9781629212883

Printed in the U.S.A

Cover illustration and design by Moka Graphics and Shawn Burgo

This book is dedicated to the following people:

My husband Paul, thank you for being you. You bring sanity and clarity into our lives. You give me strength to go on. You are a devoted, wonderful, loving man and you are mine. I love you.

My sister Lori, "a bond like no other, no man and no mister can break the bond of a sister." You are my best friend, my mentor, my soul sister. You are a wonderful mother, sister, daughter and niece. I love you.

My Mom and Dad, my heart breaks for all I have put you through. I have the perfect parents. I love you.

My big brother Gregg, "Mr. Wise Guy", always quick to make light of any situation. You are a wonderful father, brother, son and nephew. I love you.

My Aunt Mary, you have been like a second Mother to me. I love you.

Aunt Fay and Uncle Jim, I hope to have made an impact on my nieces and nephews the way you did on my life!! You will always be on the forefront of my mind. I love you.

Elliott, you are my bestie! My best friend, my confident, my mentor, my listener, my gym partner and most importantly my laughing partner. All we do is laugh. What could be better? I love you.

Steven and Melanie, you have brought joy into my life, which you cannot understand until you are older. You have made me feel like your surrogate Mother. I consider the both of you as my two children. I love you.

Michelle, you are more than a friend. We are bound by an energy, the likes of which I cannot explain. I love you.

My doctors: Gary Bernstein, John Procaccino and Jeffrey Vacirca. How many patients can say they have the best team of doctors caring for them? I can. Thank you for all you do.

Author's Reflective Notes

Hello to my new readers:

This is my first publication and my life story. Take a moment and delve into the mind of "Jody".

I have had a bevy of health problems my entire life. My earliest memory is of being a 3 year old child, in the hospital with a bladder problem. I vividly remember seeing hundreds of clocks on a wall. This was due to my body temperature reading of 106 degrees, hence the hallucinating clocks. How sad is that? The earliest memory I have is being in the hospital.

I began having intestinal issues when I was 14 years old. Approximately one year later I was diagnosed with Crohn's Disease. Crohn's has been my life. It HAS defined me and made me who I am today. I should have counted all the times I was rushed to the hospital; admitted into the hospital; emergency room treatments, etc., but I didn't keep count. What would be the point? I will not receive a medal for having the most visits!

On December 22, 1991, I succumbed to a perforated bowel of the small intestine. My wedding was in six months and the doctors didn't think I would make it to my special day. Well, they were wrong. I lived to tell the tale, as well as the many other tales you will find in this book.

During the course of my life, I have been on more medication for the treatment of this debilitating disease, than I care to admit to. This medication was so powerful, I was told to delay having a family, due to genetic mutations that could occur with the fetus. My husband is nine years older than I, so I wanted to start a family as quickly as I could. To compound matters even more, I wanted five children. What was I going to do? So I waited. And waited. And waited, until I couldn't have children, nor, at that point, did I want children. Being constantly sick, really sick, how could I care for another being, let alone a baby?

Fast forward to February 2012. I really didn't feel well. I was in and out of the hospital many times from April through August 2012. On August 30, 2012 I had a series of diagnostic tests performed, which ultimately lead to emergency surgery with a diagnosis of Small Bowell Adenocarcinoma. Life went from bad to worse. Surgery, infection, blood transfusion, chemotherapy, etc. etc. etc. But, life is good. I am here to tell my story.

Throughout my life I have used humor to cope with tragedy. Why cry when you can laugh? The ironic part about this book is NOTHING IS FUNNY! These poems are based on real life events, real life motivation, real life determination and real life lessons. Use this book to heal yourself and unearth the real you. You are more resilient than you know.

I have written this book in "reader friendly" context. You will not require a literary degree to understand this book. When reading Angles and Ogres, take note of the double-entendre's and pay particular attention to the hidden numbers sprinkled throughout the book. These numbers are significant to me. See if you can find them and guess at their meaning.

On copy printed versions, the back of every poem contains a page entitled,

"Reflective Notes". Take a moment to jot down your immediate thoughts upon reading the poems. For all e-readers, please take advantage of the notes feature on your device.

I hope you enjoy reading Angles and Ogres as much as I have enjoyed writing it.

Table of Contents

Chapter One

Thought Provoking

This chapter is my favorite. "Deep" and "reflective" are some of the words I have heard people say. Thought provoking says it all!!!

ANGELS AND OGRES

Do you walk with an angel on your right
    shoulder
Or an ogre on your left?
Do you say, "good morning"
Or do you scowl and beat your chest?

As an angel,
You are pure of heart with good intentions
Judge wisely and with discretion
An aura of radiant light
Ever shining so bright

As an ogre,
You are cruel and wicked
Evil is transmitted
Through your pores and cracks
As you commit unrighteousness acts

Are you a little of both?
In an instant, you are as angelic as a rose
With the turn of time, you hate yourself
    and loathe
Of this you must admit
Nothing but a mere hypocrite

Jody Mitchell

Angel or ogre?
How do you walk this life
And who's on your shoulder?

Reflective Notes

BAD THINGS

Bad things happen to good people
Whether you are strong willed or feeble
No one deserves for bad events to
   take place
You must handle it, with grace

Live your life day to day
Open the door and make way
Don't wait for that wake-up call
Live life to the fullest, above all

Make peace with people, do not hold any
   grudges
In the end, only God has the final say and
   judges
Get your priorities straight
Abandon jealousy and hate
Family always comes first
For they have seen you at your best and
   your worst

In life bad things will take place
How will you deal with it and win the race?

A poor decision, is one made without
   wisdom
A wise decision and you have risen
To meet life head on
You will rise to meet the dawn
You have clearly won

Reflective Notes

_____

_____

_____

_____

_____

_____

_____

BADGE OF HONOR

What do you wear as your badge of honor?
Do you wear it like a suit of armor?
Or do you wear it with a meek and timid
   demeanor?

Your badge of honor could be a medal or
   a scar
Your crown of glory or a shooting star
How you wear your badge will depend
On how you came to terms and made your
   amends

If you have received your badge of honor in
   the war
You have proven, you deeply care for
Your fellow man
For which you took the stand
You protect and defend
Your country and Mother land

If your badge of honor is a scar
It is your beacon, your North Star
Do not try to hide, what was cast upon you
Be steadfast, tried and true

You should never hide what you have earned
And you should never be concerned
About what others may think
Even if they analyze you like a Shrink

How you wear your badge will define
On the grace and elegance in which you
   crossed the finish line
Whatever your badge is, wear it with glory
And live life to tell the story

Reflective Notes

_____

_____

_____

_____

_____

_____

_____

CLOUDY DAY

Never give in to dismay
Good things can happen on a cloudy day

Good things can happen on a cloudy day
A wedding has occurred; the bride has
    tossed her bouquet
A marriage has formed, a bound union
This glorious day is not in ruin

Good things can happen on a cloudy day
A home is purchased, the contract is
    signed away
The couple moves in, while it pours with rain
Memories are made, etched in your brain

Good things can happen on a cloudy day
With the gentle cooing of a morning dove
A child is conceived out of love
Your life has an about turn
A beautiful baby is born

Never give in to dismay
Good things can happen on a cloudy day

Reflective Notes

DISASTERS

There are all kinds of disasters
For which we turn to our pastors
Both natural and man-made
Memories of which do not fade
Both natural and man-made
All we do is hope and pray

In Connecticut we have shootings
In New Orleans we have lootings
In the Gulf we have oil spills
Oh God, all those animals killed
Oklahoma has tornado blasters
All of these are disasters

How do we prevent this harm?
It starts with an electrical storm
Do we sound the fire alarm?
It happens so quickly, without warn
All this crazy devastation
This is an abomination

How do we prevent this harm?
He comes into our school with firearms
Do we engage and try to disarm?

It happens so quickly, without warn
This deadly intrusion
Can only have one conclusion

Please keep our children safe
Free from harm and unscathed
Please protect our farm and home
When destruction hits, we will roam
Protect us from these disasters
When they hit, we pray to the Master

Jody Mitchell

Reflective Notes

_____

_____

_____

_____

_____

_____

_____

DO YOU REMEMBER WHEN

I sometimes think
About life's moments that passed by in a
    blink
Do you remember when
You last held your child's hand?
Or when you took that last walk
With your beloved making small talk
Taking for granted these snippets of time
Moments relived in your mind

Do you remember when
Your life begun?
What is your earliest memory,
Of your life as a baby?
Why do we forget these formative years
When we laughed, cried and shed tears

Do you remember when
You met your best friend?
Did you meet in school
And did you both break the rules?
Is your best friend still around?

Have you kept in touch or do they bring
  you down?
Do you remember when
You lost your best friend?

Do you remember when
You met the love of your life?
Did he prove worthy, or was she your wife?
Did your love and devotion
Move like the tides of the ocean?
Over the dozens of years, as your marriage
  grew
When did you last say, "I love you?"

Do you remember when
You drew your final breath
And left this world, in a glorious death?

Reflective Notes

_____

_____

_____

_____

_____

_____

_____

DREAM

I have a reoccurring dream
Of a fantasy place
Where Grandfather Time sits and waits
Everyone remains young and of heart
Living in harmony and taking part
Of living life to its fullest
Where kindness presides without
   prejudice
Aging is eluded
Wisdom is pursued

I have a reoccurring dream
Of Mother Nature
Her resources are finite and in danger
Everyone must change their behavior
Mother Nature may wage war
Or will be our savior
Harness the power of Mother Nature's
   gifts
Wind, sun, water, to exist

I have a reoccurring dream
Of our earth
Our planet gave birth

To the creatures and animals
And all things tangible
We must preserve our earth and plan
Or it all will be destroyed by Man

I have a reoccurring dream......

Reflective Notes

_____

_____

_____

_____

_____

_____

_____

I AM YOU

I am Mother, nurturer of all
I am daughter, fruit of the tree
I am wife, partner in life
I am sister, a union like no other
I am friend, a selection process

I am the reflection in the mirror
I am you

Reflective Notes

_____

_____

_____

_____

_____

_____

_____

KIND

People are nice but they aren't kind
An email is sent, barely touching the
    surface
A greeting is extended, "how are you?"
Which, served its purpose
I am on their mind,
People are nice but they aren't kind

Your drive-way is filled with a foot of snow
They drive right by, and wave, and you
    watch them go
A door is slammed in your face
Yet, at every meal they say grace

They are the first to lead on a crusade
But it's all a masquerade
They pretend and act as if they care
Yet, behind your back, you are in their
    cross hair

They do not walk the walk
Nor talk the talk
Actions are not followed with words
Their intentions are blurred

When disaster strikes, they turn a cheek
    and are blind
They never assist man kind
They believe they are doing all that is right
How pathetic and contrite

Should you find yourself in a bind
  Just remember
People are nice but they aren't kind

Reflective Notes

_____

_____

_____

_____

_____

_____

_____

ONE BIG BREAK

In life you need one big break
One big break is all it will take
It will forever change how you view
All that is bestowed on you
If only we could have one big break
It would be icing on the cake

A big break rarely occurs
You think life is a saboteur
Never get promoted or praised
Bad luck is always engraved
On the front of your brain
Agreeing life is simply a drain

If my life had one big break
I know I'd been dreaming, not awake
One life changing moment
Could bring everlasting atonement

One big break can give you freedom
To wash away all your demons
Forever you will be grateful
An appreciation and plateful

What if you were the one to give a big break?
With one swift move, it would only take
To change someone's life in a second
You would become a name, a legend
To change someone's life forever
You made a difference in this endeavor

Reflective Notes

PATIENCE

Patience is a virtue
Of this you must pursue
It is destined in your fate
To hurry up and wait

Reflective Notes

TASK

What is the task that comes easy to you?
Find what it is and eagerly pursue
If it comes easy to you,
You must follow through
Consider it your God given talent
Use this in life to find balance

If you have to work and work for it
You must take a moment and admit
This is clearly not what you should be
    doing
Instead, you should be pursuing
Your love and passion
Find your mission

Finding your task, happens in an instance
It's something you've always done without
    resistance
Your task could be hidden; you've never
    known it to exist
But it resides in you and is your gift

If your task is your beast of burden
Call it quits, draw the curtain

You must quickly abandon
For if you do not, it will dampen
Your spirits and guiding light
Forever you will fight

Find your true calling
And you will be applauding
The rest of your life story
Living life with glory

Reflective Notes

_____

_____

_____

_____

_____

_____

_____

TODAY

Today I will do something
And I will feel guilty
No one will save my soul or take pity
Today I did something

Today I will do something
And I will take delight in retribution
That behavior is a symptom not a solution
Today I did something

Today I will do something
And I will find contentment in his misery
Oh my God, Lord have mercy
Today I did something

Today I will do something
And I will be filled with remorse
I detoured off course
Today I did something

Today I will do something
And ask for forgiveness
I had several moments of weakness

I will pray and repent, have empathy and
   lament
Today I felt guilty about what I did
Today I did something good

Reflective Notes

TWO WORDS

Everyone always talks about those three
    little words,
But everyone forgets about the two most
    important words
Those two words are rarely said
People stay away from them with dread

Those three little words are abused
And often times, are frequently misused
It is easy to say, "I love you"
The difficult part is proving that you do

Some say those three words with ease
It rolls off their tongue, aiming to please
Like the scent of honeysuckle on a warm
    breeze
From star crossed lovers
To babies with Mothers
When those three words pass the lips
At times, it could cause a head trip

But what about those two little words?
Those are the words that can heal
Those two little words can seal the deal

Saying those words is not a sign of
   weakness
Hearing those words will render you
   speechless
All can be forgiven
If those words were spoken
Get rid of the bitterness and fury
Give in and say, "I'm sorry"

Reflective Notes

_____

_____

_____

_____

_____

_____

_____

WATER

The power of water
To cleanse and heal
To christen
To bless
To swim
To drink
Which is your use of water?

Some use water to cleanse and heal
A few solitary moments to unseal
The labors of the day are washed away

A baby is christened
The sin of being born is forgiven
The first right of passage, baby has received
   the message

A blessing of holy water has anointed the
   parishioner
You are no longer a prisoner
With the blessing of water, you are led to
   the alter

Gliding through the liquid surface

The movement of the current attains the
    purpose
Swimming through the still waters will
    never make one falter

Man cannot live without water
Colorless, odorless, tasteless
A fluid necessary for the life of animals and
    plants
Water is life
Life is for living
Living is being

Reflective Notes

_____

_____

_____

_____

_____

_____

YOUR MIND

You are pulled in so many directions
There is no down time for reflections
You are tired and hurting so badly
The mind is stronger than the body

The human body is a delicate instrument
Take care of your temple, be vigilant
In a moment's notice, your temple can
    crumble
You will falter and stumble
Your mind is stronger than your body

The human mind is a work of art
It can process data and memorize
    by heart
Your mind is creative and analytic
You are your harshest critic
Your mind is stronger than your body

In seventy years, as you sit in your
    wheelchair
You will remember events from
    long ago
As you sit in your wheelchair

You will not remember your name or
    where you are
You have a distant look and are far
Your mind caught up with your body

Reflective Notes

_____

_____

_____

_____

_____

_____

_____

Chapter Two

Olive Branch

The term "extend the olive branch" means to offer a sign of peace. I take it one step further. I titled this chapter to evoke emotions of "How have you helped? What have you done? Are you extending yourself to others?"

CHAIR

Let's chat, pull up a chair
You are filled with emotion and despair
Let me calm your soul and hold your hand
I'll nod my head and understand

The pot of tea is blowing its whistle
This is my cue and my signal
To ease your bitterness and pain
You must learn from this and attain
The courage and confidence to hold your
    head high
You must brush this aside and turn a
    blind eye

Your time will come, it's just not now
Exit the stage with a curtsy and take a bow
I hope I made you aware
Of this life moment while chatting in a chair

Reflective Notes

_____

_____

_____

_____

_____

_____

_____

FORGIVENESS

What is forgiveness?
Forgiveness is the act of excusing a mistake
Forgiveness is clear and never opaque
Instead, they hold a torch of retribution
Tormenting their soul with pollution

Vengeance is at the forefront of their mind
It never migrates and falls behind
Vengeance is held onto year after year
But over time, the details become less clear
"What did we fight about, I do not
    remember?"
Their memory fading like a smoldering
    ember

Forgiveness should not take years to master
You should move on and close this chapter
Do not hold on to vengeance and hate
Believe me when I tell you, it will abate

The good book teaches forgiveness
Do not give in to weakness
Start a new story and begin
To forgive everyone and everything

Reflective Notes

_____

_____

_____

_____

_____

_____

_____

HE NEEDED A GOOD COOK

I know this man, I see him often
But this particular day I proceeded with
 caution
I exchanged pleasantries and wished him
 well
But something drew me back, I was
 compelled

I asked him if everything was alright
That is when he said, "Such is life"
When I further inquired about his
 statement
I saw such an upset man full of hatred

And that is when his story had begun to
 unfold
She left behind a set of twins only 4 years
 old
He told me his heart had been cut out with
 a knife
She was only 36 when The Lord had taken
 his wife

I started to cry, how could I not?
There we stood together so distraught
I will never forget what he said or how he
    looked
"The Lord took her for He needed a good
    cook"

Reflective Notes

_____

_____

_____

_____

_____

_____

_____

OLIVE BRANCH

I will continually extend the olive branch
    for peace
The alternative is waging war with no
    release
I will extend the branch with a smile on my
    face
This is a decision I made long ago and
    continue to embrace

When the branch is extended, is there a
    receiving hand?
Is the branch accepted or were you refuted
    and damned?
Turn the other cheek is what they say to do
When you turn the other cheek, you get a
    different world view

Continue to extend and turn the other
    cheek
You will stand out and be unique
Inner peace will be found, I guarantee
Extend the branch from this olive tree

Reflective Notes

_____

_____

_____

_____

_____

_____

_____

SELFISHNESS

Forget about your aches and pains
It's not all about you and your complaints
Forget about your personal trials and
    tribulations
There's more to life than you and your
    expectations
People are consumed with them and their
    own
Living in a glass house and throwing stones

Get yourself off your own mind
Go out and help mankind
Go find someone who needs support
Support should be natural and comes from
    the heart

Be kind to yourself but be kinder to others
For you do not know the path they have
    walked
Their hurdles or stumbling blocks

Who have you helped of late?
Did you do it with love or with hate?
If you helped someone as an obligation

You will not find salvation
If you helped someone with good
    intentions
You will have found a new dimension

Reflective Notes

_____

_____

_____

_____

_____

_____

_____

WANT AND NEED

How much do you really need?
It's not how much do you want,
It's how much do you need?
Once you find the answer, you must take
  heed

If all you do is wish for more,
You will continue to be poor
What are you doing to further yourself?
Only you can obtain your wealth

If all you do is want,
You will be left looking gaunt
If you act with greed,
You'll spend it all, leaving you to bleed
What a fool you've been,
Blowing it all, what a sin

How much do you need?
Pay for colleges, pay your bills
Give it away, give people chills
How much do you need?
If you believe in the bible, adhere to the
  Creed

Jody Mitchell

Love and God will take care of the rest
And give life with new seed

Now you know what you need,
Don't give in to any kind of greed
Know your strengths, know your loves
Life will come to you with peace and doves

Reflective Notes

_____

_____

_____

_____

_____

_____

_____

Chapter Three

Soul Squisher

I titled this chapter for any and all bad luck that just happens to occur and to all those party poopers and dream squashers. I may receive bad news, but I will never give up. People may thrust their negativity at me, but I will never let them influence my emotions! Events in your life, as well as people in your life, can sometimes be "soul squishers." Identify, refute, and persevere.

ANGRY

Why are these people so angry?
They are irrefutably unhappy
Why are they filled with rage?
Like pent up animals pacing in a cage

Some people will always be troubled
They will burst every single bubble
Good news is always turned around
Every smile becomes upside down
Bad decisions have always been made
A life of entitlement portrayed

They have lived their life
And they have paid a price
They believe something is owed to
    them
It is all that is spoken about again
    and again

The chip on their shoulder
Is the weight of a boulder
The anger grows heavier with each
    passing day
It is never far and always at bay

Anger and resentment have consumed
Who they are, forever entombed
In this shell of a body
Always angry

Reflective Notes

_____

_____

_____

_____

_____

_____

_____

LIFE ON EARTH

Are You punishing me?
Or have you opened my eyes and set me
    free?
I am continually a witness
To such bliss and unhappiness
In questioning Your existence

I understand I will find my peace in eternity
But right now I'm on this earth and not in
    harmony
I have been put on this earth to suffer
And life seems tougher
When I'm thrown grenades
Each and every day

It is difficult to remain optimistic
When I feel life is being sadistic
It is hard to turn my cheek
When my life is grim and bleak
At every turn, there is always despair
Pardon me, are You even there?

I frequently preach and praise the Lord
But it is hard when I don't hold the trump
   card
My story is being told for me
I do not hold the key
With every turn, matters are out of my
   hands
I just don't understand

My wants are few
My needs are even less
But I must confess
This daily grind is leaving me exhausted
Has my mind been accosted?
Has the devil wormed his way in?
And have I sinned?

My devotion cannot abate
I must await my fate
Though my life on earth may seem so long
I must remain strong
In reality, life is merely a number of decades
Whereas, eternity is forever

Reflective Notes

_____

_____

_____

_____

_____

_____

_____

PROVE YOURSELF

I am forever proving I am worthy
I am judged without mercy
Do they have it in for me and are they haters?
Or is this just human nature?

What makes individuals criticize and cast
    their venom?
They spew it like their personal weapon
Are they this devilish to their family?
Or do they stalk randomly?
Smelling their prey at will,
Always in for the kill

I am forever proving I am worthy
Always meeting controversy
Why am I singled out?
Each and every time I am kicked about
But I rise to the occasion
I confront the serpent's invasion
I am ready for this battle
Fending off their bite and rattle

Tomorrow will bring another round
Of proving myself on this hunting ground

Reflective Notes

_____

_____

_____

_____

_____

_____

_____

THE CALL

It was late September
And I will always remember
This point in time
When my life changed, while in my prime

At first I didn't hear the phone ring
I was too busy showering
I wasn't aware I would receive the call
The world suddenly seemed so small

The doctor and I exchange small talk
He tells me the news and I'm in shock
He proceeds to tell me the results and
    answer
He explains it is cancer

Cancer does not discriminate
You can't expect or anticipate
Is this a stroke of luck or a twist of fate?
Some consider cancer to be a life changing
    event
Others consider it pure torment

But you need to look on the brighter side
This is the defining moment, the great
  divide
To put your best foot forward
To live without borders
For you answered the call
And lived to tell about it all

Reflective Notes

_____

_____

_____

_____

_____

_____

_____

THIS DAY

Every day of your life is a celebration
Stand up; put your hands together in
    ovation
Do not memorialize a date with sadness
This day should be recognized with
    gladness

People honor a date and time of death
When their loved one took their final
    breath
They focus on their last goodbye
Why not acknowledge all the days they
    were alive?

People honor a date and time of a fateful
    call
When suddenly their world seemed so
    small
Their soul cut open with a knife
Why not acknowledge this was the call that
    saved your life?

Do not let a date lead you astray
Instead memorialize this day

Reflective Notes

_____

_____

_____

_____

_____

_____

_____

Chapter Four

Abba, Adonai, Advocate, Allah, Almighty, Alpha, Buddha, Creator, Chosen One, Christ, Commander, Divine, Elohim, God Almighty, Jehovah, Master, Noble, Nobleman, The Lord, Yahweh

I titled this chapter with all the names I could think of for "God". This chapter has everlasting faith and devotion.

I AM GOING TO BUILD A HOUSE

I am going to build a house
And dedicate it to Almighty God
Where we will praise and applaud
The teachings of The Lord

I am going to build a house, made of mortar
   and brick
All parishioners will be transfixed
With the beauty of The Lord
Who resides in this house of mortar and
   brick
All Sins are washed away and kicked

I am going to build a church of steel
Parishioners pray and kneel
No man shall ever wonder
No soul torn asunder

I am going to build The Lord a dwelling
Where scripture is read and ever
   compelling
Gospel is sung, Preachers preach

The word of The Lord never far or out of
    reach

I am going to build a home in my heart
Where goodness is found and evil depart
I am going to build a home in my heart, for
    The Lord
He will forever bless me and reward

Reflective Notes

_____

_____

_____

_____

_____

_____

_____

JUDGEMENT DAY

When it is judgment day
You do not have a vote or a say
Only The Lord can make a decision
And deem if you are forgiven

One cannot be judgmental
In The Lord's eyes, this is detrimental
Be kind and gentle with your word
For you reside in the house of The Lord

Walk in the righteous path
Stray far from vengeance and wrath
Cast not your judgment
Or you will forever be plagued with
   torment

You must not wield your sword
For you are not The Lord
Who are you to cast the final decision?
Lest we forget, we are Christian

If Judgment Day occurs
One must be assured
The Lord will descend

He will condone or condemn
But only He will make that decision
For we are the children
Of Jesus Christ
We must never be enticed
To pass judgment
On our fellow brethren

Reflective Notes

_____

_____

_____

_____

_____

_____

_____

PEACE

Depart from evil and do good deeds
Seek peace every day and you will succeed
Make peace a priority in life
Don't give in to stress and strife
Do this now and you will be saved
The road is golden and paved

You are the dictator of your agenda
You and only you can surrender
Seek calmness and clarity
Donate and give to charity
To yourself, don't over commit
If you add this burden, you won't benefit

Seek, inquire for, crave peace and pursue
As dictated by Scripture, you have virtue
God points us in the path of success
Do you follow or ignore and digress?

Obtain the essential fruit called, "peace"
You will have a new life and lease
Start viewing your life as priority
You and only you are the authority
To make this permanent alteration

Make this change and you will have
   completion

Peace, peace, peace be with you
Live stress free, and He will be with you

Reflective Notes

_____

_____

_____

_____

_____

_____

_____

SEEDS OF FAITH

Upon Jesus' Crucifixion and Resurrection
The disciples acted as missionaries
Spreading the seeds of faith
Venturing far and wide
Meeting resistance and being cast aside

Paul of Tarsis became an apostle after Jesus'
    death
On his journey, he praised Jesus until his
    last breath
Paul wrote half of the letters in the New
    Testament
He turned away from sin and repent

When all else disappears
Faith, hope and love remain
Jesus has anointed us and ordained
Spread the word, efforts are not in vain

Paul said, "love is patient, love is kind,
Love is not jealous, love does not boast,
Suffering produces perseverance,
Perseverance creates character,
Character is hope"

His dying wish, he continued to save
And sowed the seeds of faith

Reflective Notes

_____

_____

_____

_____

_____

_____

_____

THE GATE

Jesus speaks of two different ways;
The broad way and the narrow way
Which path will you use?
How will you choose?

The broad way is wide open
The path is clearly golden
But what lies ahead
Has been misread
For the broad way is evil,
It is devious and deceitful
You succumb to anger and vengeance,
Bitterness and resentment
The path way was wide
You have been cast aside

The narrow way is restricted
The path is clearly limited
But what lies ahead
Can never be misread
The narrow way leads to life
The Spirit resides in you without strife
You have chosen wisely
Praise God Almighty

Emotions make us choose the easy way,
The broad way
Wisdom makes us choose the hard way,
The narrow way

Reflective Notes

_____

_____

_____

_____

_____

_____

TURN TO THE LIGHT

The key to victory is to cast down wrong
    thoughts
Search within and turn to the Cross
The only road to true happiness is positive
    thinking
Step fiercely to the alter, instead of shrinking

Seek out the written word
Scripture is clear, not blurred
Seek shelter within and look to the Lord
Have everlasting faith, never get bored

Redeem yourself from sin
You will find peace therein
Only He can make things better
Only He can bring lives together

Get rid of the darkness
Turn to the light
Learn the difference
Between wrong and right

Be grateful for what you have
For God is good

Sometimes His direction is misunderstood
The path is not always clear to us
Never lose faith and never fuss
For in the end it is always clear
There was nothing to have feared
Look to a higher Being
Give way to negativity and freeing
Always remember,
Believers are achievers

Reflective Notes

_____

_____

_____

_____

_____

_____

_____

VOICES

When God speaks, it is a mere whisper
It is not written, like Scripture
There are no bolts of lightning, or claps of
   thunder
It is a quiet encounter
You must be listening closely
If you hear it, you will be set free
you may miss it, if you're not paying
   attention
When you hear it, you have eternal
   redemption

Turn your ear to The Lord
And listen to His word
That is gently spoken
Let your mind be open
Pay heed to His voice
For you have a choice

What are the voices you hear?
Do you go willingly or do your fear?
God speaks in many ways
Lift up your head and raise
Your hands to God and praise

God's voice may come in, on a gentle breeze
When it is heard, you have the key
To open your mind and do God's task
To revel in the glory and bask
In God's eternal love
For it came to you on a gentle breeze,
And it has set you free

Reflective Notes

_____

_____

_____

_____

_____

_____

_____

WORK IN PROCESS

I am a work in process
Please help me address
That I come to you with flaws
I turn to you for guidance above all

Have patience with me dear Lord,
For I am a work in process
I'm trying to read Your signs
But at times I am blind
I cannot see Your forest through the trees
"Lord, give me sight", while I pray on both
    knees

Have patience with me dear Lord,
For I am a work in process
I'm trying to listen to Your word
But at times my hearing is impaired
I cannot hear Your guiding instruction
"Lord, let me hear so I may part from
    corruption"

Have patience with me dear Lord,
For I am a work in process
I'm trying to walk in Your righteous path

But at times my legs are too heavy
With each and every
Step that I take, my legs ache
"Lord, give me strength, so I may walk this
    path at length"

Have patience with me dear Lord,
For I am a work in process
Give me sight, give me sound, give me
    strength

Reflective Notes

Chapter Five

I'm My Biggest Fan

If you don't love yourself, who will? This chapter is all about what "I" can do and the most important person to rely on is me!

ACKNOWLEDGE, EMBRACE, ACCEPTANCE

I was fraught with adversity my entire life
I never met a single path without strife
I learned from a tender young age
That with each encounter you must turn
the page

When the road gets rough
You must remember this expression
Acknowledge, embrace, acceptance
It will release you, it will teach confidence

This trio is similar to the 12 steps
This is not easy, but complex
If you follow through, until the end
You will be set free, not condemned
Live with it, learn from it

Acknowledgement is step one
Think, think, and think, until you are done
You have identified your problem,
You have done it and are up to the
challenge

Embrace is step two
You must fully engage, until you break
   through
It is difficult to embrace what you hate
But you must be truthful, you must be
   straight

Acceptance is step three
Acceptance, acceptance, it will set you free
You must live for this moment
You will reflect, you will prevail, and you
   are not broken
Acceptance, acceptance, you have been put
   through the test
Acceptance, acceptance, you are now
   perfect

Reflective Notes

_____

_____

_____

_____

_____

_____

_____

ALONE

I am surrounded by family and friends
I am the party planner who always pretends
How to have good times and plenty of fun
But I have this weight on my shoulders, as
    heavy as 2 tons
I am surrounded by people all the time
But I always feel alone saying, "I'm fine"

I am always putting on a strong face
Getting ready for the next blow and I brace
Looking into the eyes of adversity
But inside I am screaming, "help me!!!"
Do they really think I cannot be broken
Just because I do not say my feelings and
    remain unspoken?

My family is here, they have my back
I have my dogs and my cat
They do not know I feel so alone
If I told them how I felt, they would
    condone
But I feel I am fading to black
Having what is known as a "panic attack"

I say, "I'm fine" but look into my eyes,
When you look, what do you see?
You should see it's all a disguise and realize
That sometimes it's hard just to be alive

Friends do not want to hear I am not doing
    well
If they did, they would run away from me
    and repel
Friends just want to laugh and have a good
    time
That's why I always say, "I'm fine"
At the end of the day, I have always known
That through it all I am always alone

Reflective Notes

_____

_____

_____

_____

_____

_____

_____

CRISIS

When a crisis strikes,
Do you know who your friends are?
Are they near or are they far?
Friends are quick to say,
"I am here for you, I am your rock"
To your dismay and shock
As the earth is round
They were nowhere to be found

Friends you have had for umpteen years
Have abandoned you with your fears
No one was there to hold your hand
Who would have seen this coming or
    planned
For your friends to have deserted
Leaving you rejected and disconcerted

When you are plagued with a crisis
It is up to you and your devices
To cope with the situation
You are in for the long hall, the duration
When a crisis strikes
It is up to you to win the fight

Now you know who your friends are
And who your friends are not
Words of wisdom and food for thought
Friends will come and go
Leaving you to show
You are better than them
You will never condemn

Reflective Notes

_____

_____

_____

_____

_____

_____

_____

GLIMPSE

I had a glimpse of the future today
We were driving very far away
Trying to outrun our demons
They relentlessly pursue us for no reason

I had a glimpse of the future today
The clouds above were dark and gray
Nations were fighting and at war
They wanted to draw blood and settle the
    score

I had a glimpse of the future in my dream
We were picnicking by the lovely stream
There was peace and harmony in our mind
Demons and war did not define
Who we are as a person or nation
This is not our extermination

I had a glimpse of the future
And I was not the loser

Reflective Notes

_____

_____

_____

_____

_____

_____

_____

ME, MYSELF AND I

Each day newly anointed
Each day disappointed
Doesn't anyone follow through on their
      pledge?
Let downs always etched
Into the farthest reaches of my mind
Disappointment always redefined

A promise is made
Words exchanged in serenade
A promise is broken
Words unspoken
A promise unfulfilled
The damage is done, I must rebuild

A date and time is set
Cancellation occurs without regret
It's okay, I'll restore order
I'll do it willingly, not like a martyr
Continually tending to "damage control"
The promise breakers have no heart or soul

And yet again
I can always rely
On me, myself and I

Reflective Notes

_____

_____

_____

_____

_____

_____

_____

Chapter Six

The Climb

At your darkest, lowest moment, you and only you must climb up and out of your despair. YOU are responsible for your happiness. YOU are responsible for your actions. YOU must put one foot in front of the other, for that climb.

BRAVE

I learned from an early age
That I must be brave
Being courageous and bold
Can be both negative and positive, all told

The terrifying emotions of being afraid
Roll through your body and cascade
Being fearful
Will bring an endless tearful

For the sake of my loved ones
I roll with the punches as they come
I act seemingly stoic
This undertaking is heroic

My eyes have seen more than enough in so
    few years
This is my story, I did not volunteer
Where does my bravery come from, I am
    not aware
It's an endless bounty always on the breath
    of a prayer

Reflective Notes

_____

_____

_____

_____

_____

_____

_____

EVERY DAY

With every ounce of my being
And my last breath
I will always say,
"God, keep me from harm and protect me
    every day"

I am going out into that jungle
People are watching and hoping I stumble
But my footing is firm,
I am not short term
I am in for the long haul
They will never see me fall

Harm surrounds us in every way
But you must never delay
To hope for the best
And never digress
Into the vortex of despair
Saying, "Life's not fair"

Each and every day
I will always pray
For God to keep me from harm
I will profess and confirm

My hope for a civilized nation
And people of the same vocation

I have faith and love
In God above
I know my Maker and my call
I am love and I have it all

Reflective Notes

IF YOU KNEW

If you knew what life had in store for you
Would you want to know?
Do you think that knowledge
Would stunt you or would you grow?

If you use this knowledge to cheat the
    system
You are far from the mark and distant
Your actions are demented and blunted
You are unmistakably stunted

If you use this knowledge that had been
    foretold
Of your life that would unfold
You used every moment as a stepping stone
You have obviously grown

This epic novel is your life story
The good, the bad, the endless worry
You looked back on your years
And did not change a single day
It has made you who you are
You do not feel betrayed

Reflective Notes

_____

_____

_____

_____

_____

_____

_____

THE JOURNEY

It was decided for me, a journey I must take
The path must be traveled, without mistake
My faith was tested and I questioned "why?"
I looked up to the heavens and cried,
"If you hear me oh Lord, please don't let me
    die."

I have too much to live for, please don't
    take it away
I'll do anything I can, just to live another
    day
I discovered a new strength about me,
A strength I had never known
From this journey
I have grown

I am determined
I am a rock
This is my journey
A mere stumbling block

Reflective Notes

_____

_____

_____

_____

_____

_____

_____

TURN THE PAGE

It is easy to dwell on life's misery
You have lost your focus and are empty
Every day brings more of the same
You are constantly looking at someone to
    blame

You toss and turn in bed without a dream
But, when you arise at dawn, the plate is
    wiped clean
With each waking day you must give way
Do you forget about yesterday?
Or do you live for tomorrow?

Let go of the past in order to grasp the
    future
In order to close this chapter,
You must turn the page

Reflective Notes

_____

_____

_____

_____

_____

_____

_____

WHERE YOU WERE MEANT TO BE

So many times, I hear people say
"I didn't think my life would be this way"
A decision has already been made
We just don't know the answer
We can question, "Why" but
Life has its own chart, life is the master

Do you ever just wonder about your
   existence?
Are you meeting life with resistance?
Do you question where you should be,
Versus where you actually are?
Does your answer elude you like a shooting
   star?

A course has been charted, where do we
   point the wheel?
Turn to the right, you get a raw deal
Turn to the left and it is surreal
You must live in the moment
You must live day to day
You can't question Him and say

"Why did my life turn out this way?"

"Be careful what you pray for", that's what
    they say
Answered prayers are met with tears
    everyday
At any age, you are in a position
To accept where you are at and your
    mission
You may not be where you thought you
    would be,
But, you are where you were meant to be

Reflective Notes

_____

_____

_____

_____

_____

_____

_____

Jody Mitchell

WHY NOT?

I never questioned, "why me?"
What I did question was, "why not me?"
Why should my burdens be passed on,
To some unsuspecting John?
My shoulders must carry this burden
Of this, I am certain

My burden is mine to bear
It weighs heavy on my soul and tears
I am weary, day after day
But I never stray
These problems are mine
I don't wish them on anyone, I resign
To the fact, that I will toe the line

I can carry this load, for my shoulders are
    strong
But at times, I wish and long
For a lighter load to carry
Forever praying to the Virgin Mary
Continue to bless me with willpower
And crush every encounter
Never questioning, "why me?"
Forever saying, "why not me?"

Reflective Notes

_____

_____

_____

_____

_____

_____

Chapter Seven

Enough

At what point do you determine that you have had enough? If your sponge is fully saturated and cannot withstand another drop, this chapter is dedicated to you.

ANCHOR

Who is your anchor?
Does he ground you or does he hamper?
Does he keep you from flying away,
Or does he stoke the flames to your dismay?

What is your anchor?
Is it booze or drugs, the alluring enchanter?
Perhaps it is the comfort of mindless eating
Always starting anew, always cheating

Where is your anchor?
Look in the mirror and answer
"I will be fine; I must slice this anchor line."

Reflective Notes

_____

_____

_____

_____

_____

_____

_____

CUT THE LINE

When I close my eyes for the very last time
I will put one foot in front of the other, for
   that final climb
When I reach the heavens above
I will look fondly on my life, something to
   be proud of

But, I have questions which must be asked
Finally, some answers at long last
What is this I see in front of my eyes?
No, no, this cannot be, it must be a disguise
Low and behold at the pearly gates
Hundreds and hundreds of souls await

My earthly body has been abused and
   battered
A life time of dreams shattered
A roller coaster of emotions over dozens of
   years
Resulting in thousands upon thousands of
   tears

On earth I have done my time
And now in heaven I will cut the line

Reflective Notes

_____

_____

_____

_____

_____

_____

_____

LINE IN THE SAND

What is your defining moment?
Can you give a clue or hint?
When do you say you have had enough?
Or do you endure and prove you are tough?

No one can tell you or advise
Only you can make this decision and decide
Do you put an end to this and take a stand
Or do you give in to the demands

You can destroy your life with your own hand
Now It is time to draw a line in the sand

Reflective Notes

_____

_____

_____

_____

_____

_____

_____

MY BEST

When I do a job, I give it my all
If it's not good enough, oh well
I gave it my best, you don't get any more
I humbly request and implore
Understand where I'm coming from
Don't look down on me, I'm not dumb

If you are not happy with the way it
    turned out
Don't turn this on me and give me
    self-doubt
I gave it my all, and I don't recall
Any stresses and demands
You didn't lend a helping hand
All you do is criticize and slam
Who are you, the high command?

I can't give you more than my best
And to this I will attest
My best is my best
You don't get to protest
I've done everything I'm able
This is the truth and no fable

Jody Mitchell

I gave it my all, my best
I can't give you more than my best
I said it all, I've professed
I am driven with devotion
And no amount of emotion
Will deflate or depress
For I gave it my best

Reflective Notes

_____

_____

_____

_____

_____

_____

_____

CPSIA information can be obtained at www.ICGtesting.com
Printed in the USA
BVOW05s1602130214

344802BV00004B/4/P